DO YOU REALLY WANT TO MEET
A CROCODILE?

WRITTEN BY CARI MEISTER   ILLUSTRATED BY DANIELE FABBRI

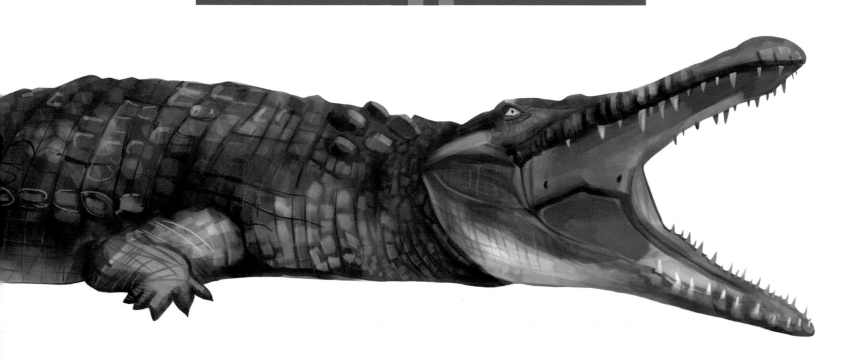

Amicus Illustrated is published by Amicus
P.O. Box 1329, Mankato, MN 56002
www.amicuspublishing.us

Library of Congress Cataloging-in-Publication Data
Meister, Cari, author.
 Do you really want to meet a crocodile? /
Cari Meister ; illustrated by Daniele Fabbri.
   pages cm. — (Do you really want to meet?)
 Summary: "A child goes on an adventure to
Australia in search of the largest crocodile and
learns about the dangers of these wild reptiles"—
Provided by publisher.
 Includes index.
 ISBN 978-1-60753-457-0 (library bound) —
ISBN 978-1-60753-672-7 (ebook)
1. Crocodiles—Juvenile literature. 2. Australia—Juve-
nile literature. I. Fabbri, Daniele, illustrator. II. Title.
 QL666.C925M455 2015
 597.98'2—dc23   2013036947

Editor: Rebecca Glaser
Designer: Kathleen Petelinsek

Printed in the United States of America at
Corporate Graphics in North Mankato, Minnesota.
10 9 8 7 6 5 4 3 2 1

ABOUT THE AUTHOR

Cari Meister is the author of more than 120 books for children, including the *Tiny* series and *My Pony Jack*. She lives in Evergreen, CO and Minnetrista, MN with her husband, John, their four sons, one dog, one horse, and 4 hamsters. You can visit her online at www.carimeister.com.

ABOUT THE ILLUSTRATOR

Daniele Fabbri was born in Ravenna, Italy, in 1978. He graduated from Istituto Europeo di Design in Milan, Italy, and started his career as a cartoon animator, storyboarder, and background designer for animated series. He has worked as a freelance illustrator since 2003, collaborating with international publishers and advertising agencies.

You *say* you want to meet a crocodile—one of the fiercest predators in the world. But did you know that they have bone-crushing jaws, sharp, pointy teeth, and rough, armored scales?

And you *still* want to meet a crocodile?
Okay. Where do you want to go?
There are several crocodile species.
Maybe we should go find a dwarf caiman.

ALLIGATOR SINENSIS

DWARF CAIMAN

APAPORIS RIVER CAIMAN

GHARIAL

SALTWATER

5

What? You want to meet *that* one—the *Crocodylus porosus*?
Those crocs live in the warm waters of the Indian and Pacific oceans.

They can grow to be 23 feet (7 m) long and 2200 pounds (1000 kg).
Are you *absolutely* sure?

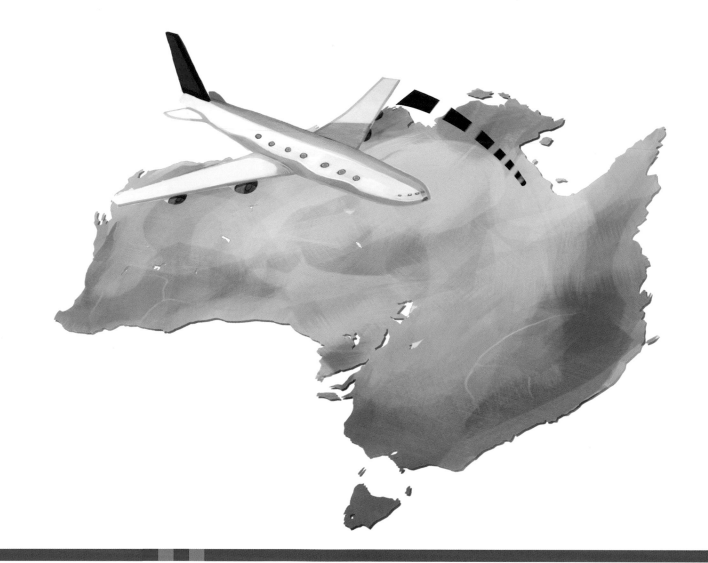

Okay, then. Pack your bags. We're off to
Northern Australia—crocodile country!

Two types of crocodiles live here—freshwater crocodiles and saltwater crocodiles. Don't let their names trick you. Both types are found in fresh and salt water—rivers, lakes, swamps, and billabongs. Anywhere there's water, there's a chance of meeting a crocodile.

freshwater crocodile

saltwater crocodile

Hold on! There are a few safety rules. After all, croc attacks on humans are rare, but they do happen.

Rule #1: Never swim **where there is a crocodile sign.**

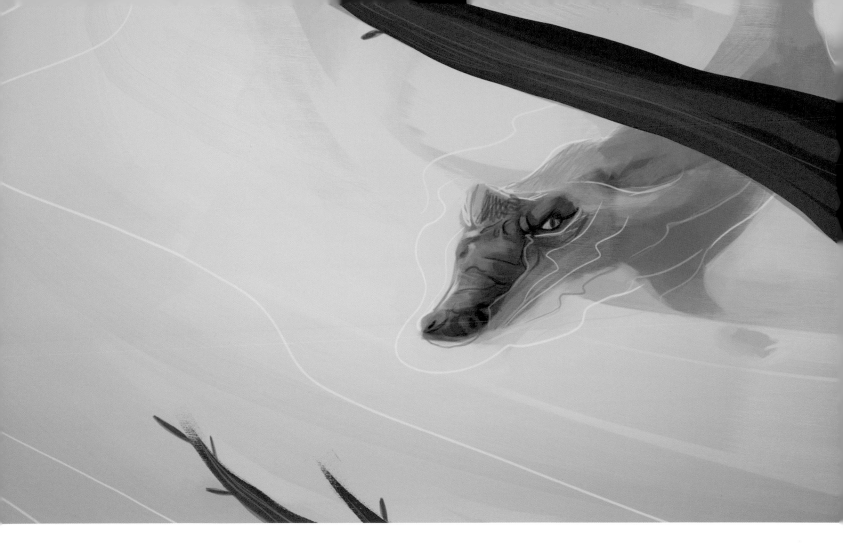

Even if you don't see a crocodile, it doesn't mean
one's not around. Crocodiles are quiet and sneaky.

Do you see that S mark? That's a crocodile sliding mark.
We must've just missed him.

Wait! Back up. Get off that ledge!

Rule #2: Stay away from ledges near water. Crocs often jump to grab their food—and you don't want to be dinner!

Yikes! That's what
I call *fast food*.

Get your hand out of the water!

Rule #3: Never dangle body parts over the edge of a boat.

Yes, I know it's hot. But crocs can hide anywhere.

See that croc with his mouth open? He's not going to attack.

His mouth is open because he's hot. Crocs can't sweat.

They open their mouths to release heat.

Rule #4: Never camp near the water.

Nope. Not here. Too close. A little further. I know you're tired. But do you want to be woken in the night by a hungry crocodile shaking the tent? No, I'm not joking. Not far from here, that exact thing happened. A couple camped too close to the water and a croc tried to get into their tent. Luckily, they escaped.

You've seen enough crocs for today. Let's go deeper into the desert, away from crocodile creek.

Perfect. We won't meet any crocs here . . .
only snakes and dingoes and lizards!

WHERE DO SALTWATER CROCODILES LIVE?

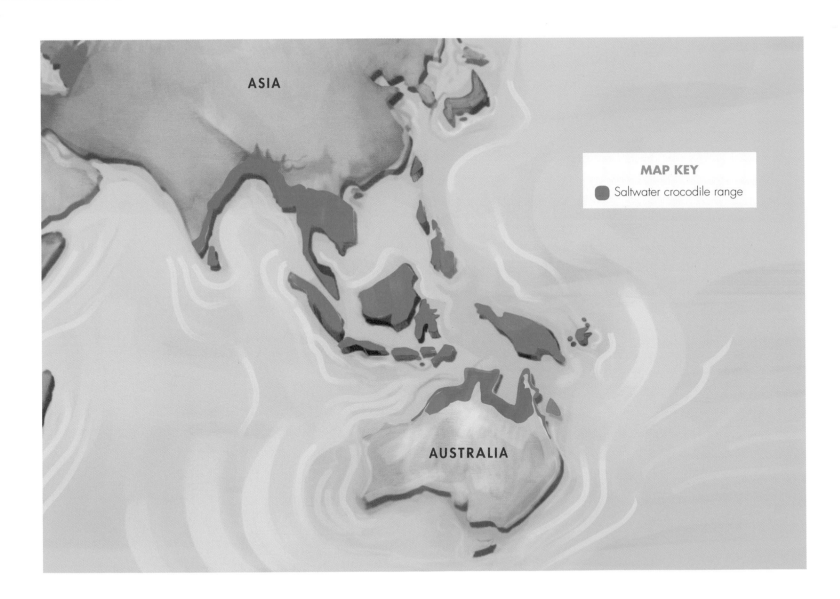

ASIA

MAP KEY

● Saltwater crocodile range

AUSTRALIA

GLOSSARY

armored scales Thin, tough, horny plates that cover some animals, like crocodiles.

billabong A dead-end channel of water.

dingo A wild Australian dog.

dwarf caiman The smallest type of crocodile in the world.

predator An animal that hunts other animals.

sliding mark The s-shaped mark crocodiles leave on the shore when they get into the water.

READ MORE

Bodden, Valerie. **Crocodiles**. Mankato, Minn.: Creative Education, 2010.

de la Bédoyère, Camilla. **Fearsome Reptiles**. Mankato, Minn.: QEB Publishing, 2012.

Saia, Stephanie. **Hunting with Crocodiles**. New York: Gareth Stevens, 2012.

Silverman, Buffy. **Can You Tell an Alligator from a Crocodile?** Minneapolis: Lerner, 2012.

Woolf, Alex. **Killer Crocodiles**. Mankato, Minn.: Arcturus, 2011.

WEBSITES

Australian Saltwater Crocodiles—Pictures and Facts
http://www.outback-australia-travel-secrets.com/saltwater-crocodiles.html
An Australian explains the dangers of saltwater crocodiles and and has pictures of them in their habitat.

Fun Crocodile Facts for Kids
http://www.sciencekids.co.nz/sciencefacts/animals/crocodile.html
Learn where crocodiles live, what makes them good hunters, how much they can weigh, and much more.

Nile Crocodile Facts and Pictures—National Geographic Kids
http://kids.nationalgeographic.com/kids/animals/creaturefeature/nile-crocodile/
Watch a video of a Nile crocodile helping her babies swim, plus read facts and see photos of these large reptiles.

Reptiles—Alligators & Crocs—Australia Reptile Park Animals
http://www.reptilepark.com.au/our-animals/reptiles/alligators-crocs/
Explore and compare pictures and facts about different species of alligators and crocodiles.

Every effort has been made to ensure that these websites are appropriate for children. However, because of the nature of the Internet, it is impossible to guarantee that these sites will remain active indefinitely or that their contents will not be altered.